Spanish for the Physical Therapist

Bridging the Communication Barrier

Asiya Nieves

Copyright © 2013 Asiya Nieves

All rights reserved.

ISBN-10: 149090154X
ISBN-13: 978-1490901541

Dedication

I dedicate this book to my grandfather, Luis "Chico" Nieves, from whom my love of Spanish was born. I also dedicate this book to you, the reader. I hope that this book helps you to better communicate with your patients.

Acknowledgements

I would like to acknowledge my family, friends, and the editors who have contributed to me being able to publish. I would like to send my deepest gratitude to my dearest friends Roslyn Dominico and Cameron Lewis for assisting me with editing in English and for their continual patience. I am indebted to Pablo Javier Accoriniti, who helped me with Spanish translation and editing, and who created the amazing cover. Pablo also helped me label the illustrations with Spanish and English titles. I would like to thank Alyssa M. Torres for doing an amazing job on the illustrations for the book. I am ever so grateful for the continued help in editing Spanish given by Fernando Caicedo Ibarra. I send my love and thanks to my brother, Isa Nieves, for allowing me to put his foot on the cover of the book, and a special thanks to Chancler Harrison for allowing me to use his beautiful hands. I send my warmest regards to Cynthia Mendoza for taking a look at my book and for helping me translate words from English to Spanish. I would like to thank Lorna Silva several times over for editing the Spanish portion of the book. And finally, I would also like to thank Shannon Olson, Sergio Bulnes, and Maria T. Carrandi for assisting me with editing.

This book could not have been published without the continued support, patience, and efforts of my family, friends, and the editors. Thank you a thousand times for helping make my dream become a reality.

TABLE OF CONTENTS

Preface IX
How to Use This Book XI

A REVIEW OF THE BASICS 1

   The Alphabet 1
   The Numbers 3
   The Days of the Week 4
   The Months of the Year 5
   Family and Friends 5
   Clothes 6
   The Parts of the House 7
   Professions 8
   Question Words 9
   Notes 10

THE BODY PARTS 11

   Anterior View 12
   Posterior View 13
   Other Body Parts 14
   Notes 15

VOCABULARY 16

    Characteristics 16
    Descriptive Adjectives 18
    Feelings & Emotions 18
    Symptoms & Complaints 20
    Pain 21
    Medical & Surgical History 22
    Directions & Positions 28
    Equipment 29
    Treatment 30
    Medical Diagnostic Imaging 31
    Movement in Medical Terminology 32
    Notes 33

EVALUATION: THE QUESTIONS 34

    Filling Out Forms 34
    Greetings 35
    General 35
    Determining Mental Status 36
    Medical and Surgical History Questions 36
    Social history 37
    Determining Equipment Needs 39
    To better Understand the Patient 40
    Determining the Problem 40
    Questions about Pain 41
    Head and Neck 44
    Shoulder 44

BACK	45
KNEE	45
CARDIORESPIRATORY	46
MUSCULOSKELETAL	46
NERVOUS SYSTEM	47
PEDIATRICS	47
RED FLAGS	49
SMOKE CESSATION	49
NOTES	50

THE EXAMINATION: MEASUREMENTS 51

THE BASICS	51
HEAD AND NECK	53
SHOULDER	53
BACK	54
KNEE	55
FOOT	55
NOTES	56

REEVALUATION: REVISIT QUESTIONS 57

REEVALUATION QUESTIONS	57
NOTES	59

PLAN OF CARE 60

MAKING AN APPOINTMENT	60
COMMANDS	61
NOTES	64

VERBS **65**

    A 65

    B 66

    C 68

    D 69

    E 70

    F 71

    G 72

    H 73

    I 73

    J 74

    K 74

    L 75

    M 76

    N 76

    O 77

    P 77

    Q 78

    R 78

    S 80

    T 82

    U 84

    V 84

    W 84

Preface

I have always had a love for the Spanish language. I took four years in high school, but did not continue studying Spanish in college, as my focus was on getting through the DPT program. Many years after I had graduated college, I began studying Spanish again when I decided to go to South America and volunteer.

In 2011, I decided to volunteer in Peru. Before my trip, I began looking for books on Spanish for physical therapy, but was unable to find any. I searched high and low, but only came across books on medical Spanish that focused on doctors and nurses. This very much frustrated me. I began going to Borders, which is now, sadly, closed, and went through books on Spanish that pertained to the medical field. I searched the internet and compiled lists of words, verbs, and phrases that could be used by a physical therapist. I began translating statements and questions into Spanish. Since I have some O.C.D. and anal tendencies, I began typing up all my notes and organizing them into what later started to resemble a book. I realized that there was a need for a book to be made after volunteering again in Ecuador in 2012, and later when I began working in California. It was then that I decided to finish writing the book and publish *Spanish for the Physical Therapist: Bridging the Communication Barrier*.

Whether you want to go overseas and volunteer or learn Spanish to speak to your patients, I hope you find this book useful. Use this book as a starting point. It is by no means complete; there are many more terms and situations that are not in this book. I just tried to capture the basics. I hope that physical therapists use this book as a guide when trying to incorporate Spanish into their practice. Therapists are encouraged to use what words work best for their patients, as there are many ways to say the same thing, and word meanings can vary by country or region. Included in this book are blank pages to add vocabulary, verbs, questions, and statements that you may find to be useful. I hope you enjoy this book as much as I have enjoyed writing it, and finally publishing it. If you have any comments, questions, or feedback, please feel free to email me at: Spanishfortherapist@gmail.com

How to Use This Book

1) The "usted" form, as the formal "you," is used in this book. The reader also has the option of using the "tú" form if you wish to be informal with your patients.

2) When a word or letter is placed in parentheses, it is used for gender changes or masculine and feminine objects. The parenthesis is also used to give the option of making a word singular or plural.

        friend - amigo(a)

So, when you are referring to a male, you use "amigo," and when referring to a female, you use "amiga."

        lo(la)

The use of the particle "lo" is for males or masculine objects, and "la" is for female or feminine objects.

3) When a word or a phrase has a bullet point underneath it, the reader should use the bullet point to complete the sentence or to further clarify a question or statement.

        Are you…? - ¿Está…?
- married - casado(a)
- single - soltero(a)

The reader can now put the sentence together in one of two ways: Are you married? <u>or</u> Are you single?

The second use of the bullet point is to clarify a statement or a question to get more details.

        Do you have pain? - ¿Tiene dolor?
- Now? - ¿Ahora?

4) The use of the ellipsis […] is also used to give the reader more options to complete the sentence. There are usually bulleted options below it, as well.

        Do you have pain when…? - ¿Tiene dolor cuándo…?
- walk - camina
- sit - se sienta

The reader can put the sentence together in one of two ways: Do you have pain when you walk? <u>or</u> Do you have pain when you sit?

5) The use of a forward slash [/] between words or phrases gives the reader the option of using either of the words or phrases.

    Are you able to drive? - ¿Puede conducir/manejar?

In this instance, the reader should choose one of the words to ask if the patient is able to drive.

    Are you able to drive? - ¿Puede conducir? <u>o</u> ¿Puede manejar?

6) The use of "or" ["o" in Spanish] between sentences or phrases gives the reader a choice on how they want to ask or say a phrase or sentence. In this book, it is also underlined to help the reader more easily identify.

    How much help did you need? <u>or</u> Did you need help? - ¿Cuánta ayuda necesitó? <u>o</u> ¿Necesitó ayuda?

7) If you come across a sentence with a series of underscores [____] you should use the bulleted words or statement to complete the sentence or question.

    Leave ____ on. - Quédese con ____ [puesta].
- the underwear - la ropa interior

The sentence would read: Leave the underwear on.

8) The use of brackets [ ] are used in this book in place of parentheses to help distinguish between the other uses of parenthesis in this book. See #2 for further clarification on the use of parenthesis.

9) At times, a *m.* or a *f.* is used to show that a word is masculine or feminine. This is only used in cases where the reader may be confused. **Please review masculine and feminine words if further clarification is needed.**

    sobrepeso *m.*

This means that sobrepeso is only masculine and cannot be made feminine. The reader cannot say sobrepesa when referring to a female.

Spanish for the Physical Therapist

Bridging the Communication Barrier

1

A Review of the Basics

The Alphabet

The following is a list of the Spanish alphabet and the proper pronunciation of the letters. It is always good to review the alphabet and learn proper pronunciation of letters and words.

Letter	Name in Spanish	Pronunciation of Name	Sound
a	a	ah	ah
b	be	beh	b like bag
c	ce	ceh	ce = s sound, th in Spain ca, co, cu = k sound
ch	che, ce hache	cheh	ch like in cheese
d	de	deh	d as in ditch
e	e	eh	sounds like ay from say
f	efe	effe	f as in fish
g	ge	hay	ge, gi = h sound ga, go, gu = hard g sound as in great
h	hache	ahchay	the h is silent in Spanish
i	i	ee	sounds like a long e as in greet
j	jota	hotah	sounds like the English h

2 | A Review of the Basics

Letter	Name in Spanish	Pronunciation of Name	Sound
k	ka	cah	k as in kite
l	ele	ellay	l as in log
ll	elle	ayyay	sounds like y in certain Spanish countries
m	eme	emmay	m as in man
n	ene	enay	n as in now
ñ	eñe	enyeh	sounds like "nio" like in onion
o	o	oh	sounds like oh [the expression oh]
p	pe	pay	p as in pat
q	coo, cu	coo	sounds like the English k
r	erre	eirray	r as in bright but pronounced as the rolling r
rr	doble erre	eirrrray	a rolling r sound but longer than the Spanish r
s	ese	esay	s as in snake
t	te	teh	t as in top
u	u	ooh	sounds like the oo of pool
v	uve	bay	the b and v sound the same in most Spanish countries
w	doble uve	dou blay bay	w as in wait
x	equis	ehkeese	ks sound between vowels, s or ks sound before another constant, and in some places an h sound like the j in Spanish **varies by region**
y	i griega	eh greeaygah	y as in yellow
z	zeta	setah	sounds like English s; in Spain sounds like th

The Numbers

1 - uno

2 - dos

3 - tres

4 - cuatro

5 - cinco

6 - seis

7 - siete

8 - ocho

9 - nueve

10 - diez

11 - once

12 - doce

13 - trece

14 - catorce

15 - quince

16 - dieciséis

17 - diecisiete

18 - dieciocho

19 - diecinueve

20 - veinte

21 - veintiuno

22 - veintidós

23 - veintitrés

24 - veinticuatro

25 - veinticinco

26 - veintiséis

27 - veintisiete

28 - veintiocho

29 - veintinueve

30 - treinta

31 - treinta y uno

32 - treinta y dos

33 - treinta y tres

36 - treinta y seis

40 - cuarenta

41 - cuarenta y uno

42 - cuarenta y dos

43 - cuarenta y tres

50 - cincuenta

60 - sesenta

70 - setenta

80 - ochenta

90 - noventa

100 - cien

101 - ciento uno

102 - ciento dos

103 - ciento tres

110 - ciento diez

120 - ciento veinte

135 - ciento treinta y cinco

147 - ciento cuarenta y siete

199 - ciento noventa y nueve

200 - doscientos

201 - doscientos uno

250 - doscientos cincuenta

263 - doscientos sesenta y tres

300 - trescientos

306 - trescientos seis

310 - trescientos diez

The Days of the Week

Monday - lunes

Tuesday - martes

Wednesday - miércoles

Thursday - jueves

Friday - viernes

Saturday - sábado

Sunday - domingo

The Months of the Year

January - enero

February - febrero

March - marzo

April - abril

May - mayo

June - junio

July - julio

August - agosto

September - septicmbre

October - octubre

November - noviembre

December - diciembre

Family and Friends

father - padre

mother - madre

son - hijo

daughter - hija

brother - hermano

sister - hermana

husband - esposo, marido

wife - esposa

grandfather - abuelo

grandmother - abuela

grandson - nieto

granddaughter - nieta

uncle - tío

aunt - tía

cousin - primo(a)

man - hombre

woman - mujer

person - una persona

boyfriend/girlfriend/fiancé - novio(a)

friend - un(a) amigo(a)

Clothes

belt - el cinturón

blouse - la blusa

bra - el sostén

button - el botón

cap - la gorra

coat - el abrigo

dress - el vestido

hat - el sombrero

high heels - los zapatos de tacón alto, los tacones altos

jacket - la chaqueta

jeans - los jeans, los vaqueros, los pantalones vaqueros

pants - los pantalones

purse - el bolso, la cartera

sandals - las sandalias

shirt - la camisa

shoelaces - las agujetas, los cordones [de los zapatos]

shoes - los zapatos

shorts - los pantalones cortos, el short, los shorts

skirt - la falda

socks - los calcetines

sweater - el suéter, la chompa

sweatshirt/sweatsuit - la sudadera

swimsuit - el bañador, el traje de baño

tennis shoes, sneakers - los

zapatos de tenis, los zapatos, los tenis

t-shirt - la camiseta

underpants - los calzoncillos

underwear - la ropa interior

uniform - el uniforme

zipper - el cierre, la cremallera, el zipper

The Parts of the House

bathroom - el baño

bedroom - el cuarto, el dormitorio, el habitación, la recámara

ceiling - el techo

dining room - el comedor

door - la puerta

floor - el piso, el suelo

garage - el garaje

garden - el jardín

hallway - la entrada, el pasillo, el recibidor

kitchen - la cocina

laundry room/washroom - el lavadero, el cuarto de lavado

living room - la sala, el salón

roof - el tejado

stairs - las escaleras, los escalones

wall - la pared

Professions

athlete - atleta

baker - panadero(a)

barber - barbero(a)

bus driver - conductor(a) de autobús

businessman - hombre de negocios

businesswoman - mujer de negocios

butcher - carnicero(a)

carpenter - carpintero(a)

cashier - cajero(a)

cleaner - encargado(a) de limpieza

clerk [office] - oficinista

clerk [retail worker] - dependiente

cook - cocinero

dentist - dentista

doctor - doctor(a), médico(a)

engineer - ingeniero(a)

farmer - agricultor(a), granjero(a)

firefighter - bombero

garbage collector - basurero(a)

hairdresser - peluquero(a), estilista

housekeeper - ama de llaves, empleada de limpieza

interpreter - intérprete

laborer - obrero

lawyer - abogado(a)

mailman - cartero(a)

mechanic - mecánico(a)

nurse - enfermero(a)

painter - pintor

plumber - plomero

policeman, police woman - policía

salesman, saleswoman - vendedor(a)

student - estudiante

teacher - maestro(a), profesor(a)

therapist - terapeuta, terapista

waiter - camarero(a)

welder - soldador

Question Words

When? - ¿Cuándo?

Where? - ¿Dónde?

To where? - ¿Adónde? o ¿A dónde?

From where? - ¿De dónde?

How much? - ¿Cuánto(a)?

How many? - ¿Cuántos(as)?

What? - ¿Qué?

Why? - ¿Por qué?

How? - ¿Cómo?

Which? - ¿Cuál?

Which ones? - ¿Cuáles?

Who? - ¿Quién? o ¿Quiénes?

From whom? - ¿De quién?

To whom? - ¿A quién?

Notes

2

The Body Parts

This section focuses on teaching the reader the names of the body parts in Spanish. The following two pages have illustrations with the body parts labeled in English and Spanish. In some instances, an English word may have more than one Spanish translation that is not listed on the illustrations. The following are examples of words with more than one Spanish translation. Please note, this is not a complete list, but it is meant to give the reader options.

buttocks - las nalgas, los glúteos, el/las pompis

cheek - la mejilla, el cachete

chin - el mentón, la barbilla

face - el rostro, la cara

hair - el pelo, el cabello

scapula [shoulder blade] - la escápula, el omóplato, la paletilla

12 | The Body Parts

Anterior View

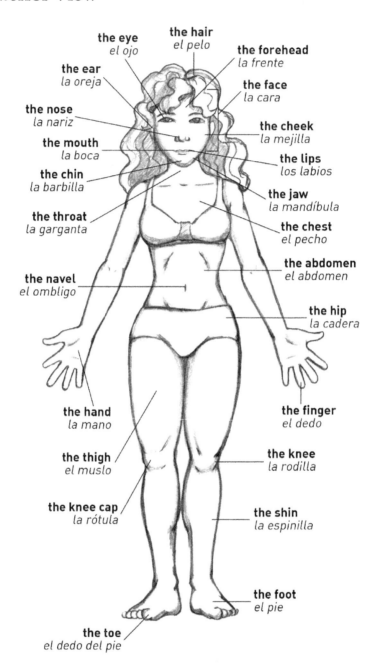

Posterior View

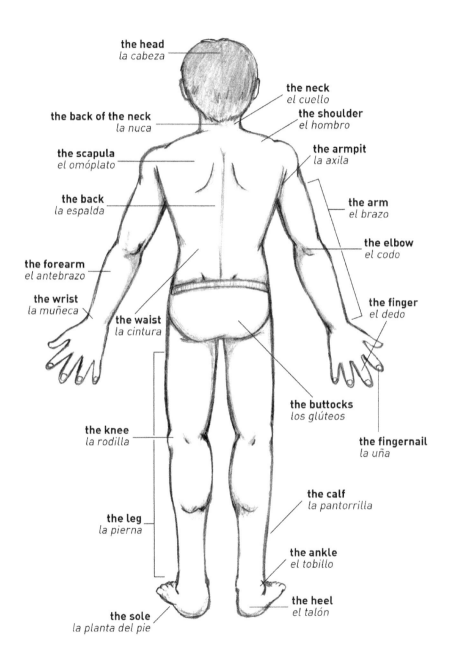

Other Body Parts

appendix - el apéndice
artery - la arteria
bladder - la vejiga
blood - la sangre
bone - el hueso
brain - el cerebro
cyst - el quiste
heart - el corazón
joint - la coyuntura, la articulación
kidney - el riñón
large intestine - el intestino grueso
ligament - el ligamento
liver - el hígado
lump/nodule - la bolita, el bulto, el nódulo
lung - el pulmón

muscle - el músculo
nerve - el nervio
pancreas - el páncreas
rectum - el recto
rib - la costilla
skeleton - el esqueleto
skin - la piel
small intestine - el intestino delgado
spine - la columna vertebral
spleen - el bazo
stomach - el estómago
tendon - el tendón
thyroid - la glándula tiroides, el/la tiroides
tissue - el tejido
vein - la vena

Notes

3

Vocabulary

This section helps orient the reader to vocabulary he or she may encounter on a day-to-day basis when dealing with patients and other healthcare providers. This section is divided into characteristics, descriptive adjectives, feelings & emotions, symptoms & complaints, pain, medical & surgical history, directions & positions, equipment, treatment, medical diagnostic imaging, and movement in medical terminology.

Characteristics

The words in this section are words that a patient may use to describe themselves or other members of their family. These words may also be used to discuss their condition or situation at home.

arrogant - arrogante

beautiful - bello(a), hermoso(a)

big - grande

charming - encantador(a)

clean - limpio(a)

clever - listo(a)

courteous - cortés

deceitful - engañoso(a)

dependent - dependiente

dirty - sucio(a)

disloyal - desleal

fat - gordo(a)

friendly - amistoso(a)

generous - generoso(a)

handsome - guapo(a)

hardworking - trabajador(a)

honest - honesto(a)

independent - independiente

intelligent - inteligente

large - grande

lazy, lazy person - flojo(a), perezoso(a)

left handed - zurdo(a), izquierdo(a)

liar - mentiroso(a)

mean - antipático(a)

new - nuevo(a)

nice - simpático(a)

obese - obeso(a)

old - viejo(a)

overweight - sobrepeso *m.*

pretty - bonito(a)

quiet - tranquilo(a)

reliable - responsable

right handed - diestro(a), derecha

serious - serio(a)

short - bajo(a)

silly, stupid - tonto(a)

sincere - sincero(a)

skinny - flaco(a)

small - pequeño(a)

tall - alto(a)

thin - delgado(a)

ugly - feo(a)

young - joven

Descriptive Adjectives

The words in this section are important in the treatment of a patient. Descriptive adjectives can help explain exercises, treatment, plan of care, etc. For example, during an evaluation of the lumbar spine, you can use the descriptive words such as "better" or "worse" to find out how different positions affect the patient's pain level.

a lot - mucho(a)	less - menos
bad - malo(a), mal	more - más
better - mejor	quick - rápido(a)
difficult - difícil	quickly - rápidamente
easy - fácil	regularly - habitualmente
few/little - poco(a)	slow - lento(a)
good - bueno(a)	slowly - despacio, lentamente
hard - duro(a)	very - muy

Feelings & Emotions

Finding out a patient's emotional status can help a therapist effectively treat a patient. For example, if a therapist finds out a patient is depressed, they can refer that patient back to their doctor or to counseling. Many patients tend to get depressed after they have had a life-altering event [e.g. a stroke or a bad diagnosis, such as multiple sclerosis]. If a patient has negative feelings, it can adversely affect treatment. For some patients, if no change is made in pain level, they may feel like they have not made any progress.

angry - enojado(a)

annoyed - molesto(a)

bad - malo(a), mal

better - mejor

cold - frío(a)

comfortable - cómodo(a)

confused - confuso(a)

curious - curioso(a)

difficult - difícil

exhausted - agotado(a)

fear - miedo *m.*

good - bueno(a)

happiness - felicidad

happy - feliz

hot - caliente

hungry - hambre

irritated - irritado(a)

nervous - nervioso(a)

pain - dolor

preoccupied - preocupado(a)

restless - inquieto(a)

sad - triste

scared - asustado(a), espantado(a)

sick - enfermo(a)

sleepy - con sueño *m.*

strange - extraño(a), raro(a)

stress - estrés

thirsty - sediento(a)

tired - cansado(a)

uncomfortable - incómodo(a)

well - bien

worse - peor

Symptoms & Complaints

This section helps the therapist identify a patient's chief complaints to help make informed decisions on the plan of care.

anxious - ansioso(a)

balance - balance *m.*, equilibrio *m.*

blurred vision - visión borrosa, vista borrosa

chills - escalofríos

cold - resfriado *m.*

confused - confuso(a)

cough - tos

cramps - calambres

depressed - deprimido(a)

dizziness - mareo *m.*

dizzy - mareado(a)

double vision - diplopía, visión doble

fever - fiebre *f.*

flu - gripe

headache - dolor de cabeza

hemorrhage - hemorragia

hypersensitivity - hipersensibilidad

infection - infección

inflammation - inflamación

knot - nudo

lethargic - letárgico(a)

migraines - migrañas

muscle spasm - espasmo muscular

nausea - náuseas

night sweats - sudores nocturnos

numbness - adormecimiento, entumecimiento

pain - dolor

painful - doloroso(a)

ringing in the ear - silbido en el oído, zumbido en el oído

sensitivity - sensibilidad

shortness of breath - falta de aire/respiración, dificultad al respirar

sneeze - estornudo

sore - adolorido(a)

spasm - espasmo

spastic - espástico(a)

sprain - torcedura

sprained - torcido(a)

stiff - rígido(a), tieso(a)

stiffness - rigidez *f.*

stomach ache - dolor de estómago

sweat - sudor

sweaty - sudoroso(a)

swelling - hinchazón *f.*

swollen - hinchado(a)

tension - tensión

tingling - cosquilleo, hormigueo

torn ligament - desgarre del ligamento, rotura de ligamento

tremors - temblores

vomiting - vómito

weak - débil

weakness - debilidad

Pain

Pain is one of the most common reasons that patients are referred to therapy. Below is a list of descriptive pain terms to help effectively treat the patient and assist with differential diagnosis.

Vocabulary

bothersome - molesto(a)

burning - ardor, ardiente, quemante

chronic - crónico(a)

constant - constante

cramps - calambres

deep - profundo(a)

dull - sordo

intense - intenso(a)

intermittent - intermitente

mild - leve

moderate - moderado(a)

numbness - adormecimiento, entumecimiento

severe - severo(a)

sharp - agudo

stabbing - una puñalada, punzante

stitch - punzada

throbbing - palpitante, pulsante

tingling - cosquilleo, hormigueo

Medical & Surgical History

Medical and surgical history gives the therapist a more comprehensive view of the patient. It also helps identify contraindications to treatment. Sometimes, patients deny medical history unless specifically asked about certain diagnoses, e.g. high blood pressure. It is therefore important to know some of the important diagnoses that can have an effect on your treatment and a patient's progress.

AIDS - síndrome de inmunodeficiencia adquirida, SIDA

allergies - alergias

Alzheimer's disease - enfermedad de Alzheimer

amputation - amputación

anemia - anemia

anxiety - ansiedad

arthritis - artritis

asthma - asma

ataxia - ataxia

attacks - ataques

Bell's palsy - parálisis de Bell, parálisis facial de Bell

blind - ciego(a)

blood clot - coágulo de sangre

blood pressure - presión arterial, presión sanguínea, presión, tensión arterial

- high blood pressure - presión alta

    e.g. 200/100 - doscientos sobre cien

- low blood pressure - presión baja

    e.g. 85/40 - ochenta y cinco sobre cuarenta

bone spurs - espolones óseos

bronchitis - bronquitis

bulging disk - protrusión de disco

bursitis - bursitis

Vocabulary

cancer - cáncer

cardiac arrest - paro cardíaco

cataracts - cataratas

cellulitis - celulitis

cerebral palsy - parálisis cerebral

cervical whiplash - lesión de latigazo, latigazo cervical, lesión de la nuca

cholesterol - cholesterol

- low cholesterol - colesterol bajo
- high cholesterol - colesterol alto

cirrhosis - cirrosis

congestive heart failure - insuficiencia cardíaca [congestiva]

coronary artery disease, CAD - enfermedad de las arterias coronarias

deaf - sordo(a)

depression - depresión

diabetes - diabetes

Down's syndrome - síndrome de Down

embolism - embolismo, embolia

emphysema - enfisema

epilepsy - epilepsia

fracture - fractura, quebradura, rotura

gall stones - cálculos en la vesícula, cálculos biliares, piedras cálculos

glaucoma - glaucoma

gout - gota

heart attack - ataque al corazón, ataque cardíaco, infarto de miocardio

heart disease - enfermedad cardíaca, enfermedad del corazón,
   cardiopatía

heart failure - insuficiencia cardíaca

heart murmur - soplo del corazón, soplo cardíaco

hemiparesis - hemiparesia, hemiparesis

hemiplegia - hemiplejía

hemiplegic - hemipléjico(a)

hepatitis - hepatitis

hernia - hernia

HIV - el virus de inmunodeficiencia humana, VIH

hyperglycemia - hiperglucemia

hypertension - hipertensión

hyperthyroidism - hipertiroidismo

hypoglycemia - hipoglucemia

kidney disease - enfermedad del riñón

kidney failure - insuficiencia renal

kidney stones - piedras/cálculos renales

leukemia - leucemia

macular degeneration - degeneración macular

multiple sclerosis - esclerosis múltiple

myocardial infarction - infarto del miocardio, infarto cardíaco, ataque cardíaco

obese - obeso(a)

obesity - obesidad

osteoarthritis - osteoartritis

osteoporosis - osteoporosis

pacemaker - marcapasos

palpitation - palpitación

paralysis - parálisis *f.*

paraplegia - paraplejía

paraplegic - parapléjico(a)

Parkinson's disease - enfermedad de Parkinson, síndrome parkinsoniano, parkinsonismo, el Parkinson

pneumonia - neumonía, pulmonía

psoriasis - psoriasis

pulmonary edema - edema pulmonar

retinopathy - retinopatía

seizure - ataque, convulsión/convulsiones

slipped disc - disco desplazado, disco desviado, hernia de disco, hernia discal, disco dislocado

spondylosis - espondilosis

sprain - torcedura

stenosis - estenosis

stroke - accidente cerebrovascular, apoplejía, derrame cerebral, infarto cerebral, embolia cerebral, hemorragia cerebral

surgery - cirugía

thrombophlebitis - tromboflebitis

thrombosis - trombosis

torn ligament - ligamento roto, desgarre del ligamento, ruptura de ligamento, ligamento rasgado

tuberculosis - tuberculosis

tumor - tumor

vertigo - vértigo

wear - desgaste

… | Vocabulary

Directions & Positions

The directions listed in this section can assist the therapist during the evaluation and treatment of a patient.

above - encima

back - atrás

backwards, towards the back - hacia atrás

behind - detrás, detrás de

below - debajo, debajo de

come here - venga aquí , venga aca

do this - haga esto

down - abajo

face down [on stomach] - boca abajo

face up [on back] - boca arriba

forward - adelante, frente

here - aquí

inside - adentro, dentro

near - cerca

next - próximo

next to - al lado de

on the left - sobre el lado izquierdo, en el costado izquierdo

on the right side - sobre el lado derecho, en el costado derecho

on top of - encima de

outside - afuera, fuera

over there - allá, por allá

pull - jale, tire

push - empuje

there - allí

to the left - a la izquierda

to the right - a la derecha

toward - hacia

up - arriba

Equipment

ankle brace - tobillera

back brace - faja

ball - pelota, bola

bedpan - chata, cuña, bacinilla

bench - banco

bike - bicicleta

cane - bastón

- three point cane - bastón trípode
- four point cane or quad cane - bastón de patitas, bastón con cuatro patas, bastón de cuatro apoyos

commode - silla con orinal

crutch - muleta

elbow brace - codera

knee brace - rodillera

mat - colchoneta

neck brace - cuello ortopédico, collar cervical

parallel bars - barra paralela, paralelas

prosthesis - miembro artificial, prótesis

roll - rodillo

sling - cabestrillo

theraband - banda elástica theraband

e.g. red theraband - banda elástica roja

treadmill - caminadora, rueda de andar, cinta de correr, trotadora

tube feeding - una sonda de alimentación

urinal - orinal

ventilator - respirador artificial, ventilación mecánica

walker - andador, caminadora, andadera

wedge - cuña

weights - pesas

wheelchair - silla de ruedas

wrist brace - muñequera

Treatment

The treatments listed in this section are medical procedures as well as therapeutic treatments.

chemotherapy - quimioterapia

continuous passive motion [CPM] machine - máquina de movimiento pasivo continuo

diathermy - diatermia

electrical stimulation/ES - estimulación eléctrica, estímulo eléctrico

- neuromuscular electrical stimulation/NMES - estimulación eléctrica neuromuscular
- transcutaneous electrical nerve stimulation/TENS - estimulación eléctrica transcutánea

hot pack - paño caliente

ice pack - compresa de hielo, bolsa de hielo

massage - masaje

radiation - radiación *f.*

traction - tracción *f.*

ultrasound - ultrasonido

Medical Diagnostic Imaging

arthrography [x-ray of joints] - artrografía

CT scan - tomografía [axial] computarizada, tomografía

echocardiography - ecocardiografía, ecocardiograma

electromyography/EMG - conducción nerviosa electromiografía, electromiografía

MRI - imágenes por resonancia magnética, imágenes de resonancia magnética, IRM, resonancia magnética

ultrasonography - ecografía, ultrasonografía, ultrasonido

X-rays - radiografías, rayos X

Movement in Medical Terminology

This section familiarizes the therapist with medical terminology. This section is not as important as the other sections in this chapter, as it is better to use layman's terminology to describe exercises or motions to patients.

abduction - abducción

adduction - aducción

dorsiflexion - dorsiflexión

eversion - eversión

extension - extensión

external rotation - rotación externa

flexion - flexión

inferior - inferior

internal rotation - rotación interna

inversion - inversión

plantarflexion - flexión plantar

pronation - pronación

superior - superior

supination - supinación

Notes

4

Evaluation: The Questions

This chapter is dedicated to helping the therapist evaluate his or her patients. It covers general questions to assist with filling out forms as well as various questions on specific body parts. This chapter does not have all the questions you may need to ask, but should be used as a guide for performing an evaluation. In this book, the "usted" form is used as the formal "you."

Filling Out Forms

Is someone here with you?	¿Está acompañado?
Please fill this out.	Por favor, complete/llene esto. Por favor, rellene esto. [Used in Spain]
Do you need help with the forms?	¿Necesita ayuda con los formularios?
Do you have health insurance?	¿Tiene seguro de salud/médico?
Your answers will help me treat your problem(s).	Sus respuestas me ayudarán a tratar su problema.

Greetings

Good...
- morning

Buenos...
- días

Good...
- afternoon
- night

Buenas...
- tardes
- noches

How are you?   ¿Cómo está?

What is your name?   ¿Cómo se llama?
¿Cuál es su nombre?

Please, spell your name.   Por favor, deletree su nombre.

I am a Physical Therapist.   Soy [un(a)] terapista físico.
Soy [un(a)] fisioterapeuta.
Soy [un(a)] terapeuta físico.

Note - You can say either, for example, Soy un(a) fisioterapeuta or Soy fisioterapeuta.

My name is...   Me llamo...
Mi nombre es...

General

Do you need an interpreter?   ¿Necesita un intérprete?

I'm here to help you.   Estoy aquí para ayudarle.

How can I help you?   ¿En qué puedo ayudarle?

Why did you come to see me?   ¿Por qué vino a verme?

Your doctor has ordered therapy for you.	Su doctor/médico ha ordenado terapia para usted.
May I ask you a few questions?	¿Puedo hacerle unas preguntas?
I am going to ask you some questions. Is this okay?	Le voy a hacer unas preguntas. ¿Le parece bien?
How tall are you?	¿Cuánto mide? ¿Qué altura tiene usted?
How much do you weight?	¿Cuánto pesa? ¿Qué peso tiene usted?

Determining Mental Status

What is your name?	¿Cuál es su nombre?
Do you know where you are?	¿Usted sabe dónde está?
Do you know what…? • day it is • month it is • year it is	¿Usted sabe qué…? • día es • mes es • año es
Why are you here?	¿Por qué está aquí?

Medical and Surgical History Questions

Are you pregnant?	¿Está embarazada?

Do you have…?
 • medical history
      ○ past
	¿Tiene…?
	 • historial médico, antecedentes médicos
	      ○ pasado(s)

- - present
  - social history
  - any surgical history

- - presente
  - historial social, antecedentes sociales
  - historial quirúrgico, alguna cirugía en el pasado, antecedentes quirúrgicos, antecedentes de alguna cirugía

Have you had…?   ¿Ha tenido…?
- any surgeries

- alguna cirugía

Do you smoke?   ¿Fuma?

Do you drink alcohol?   ¿Bebe alcohol?
¿Toma alcohol?

Do you use other drugs?   ¿Usted toma otras drogas?

Do you have problems with…?   ¿Usted tiene problemas con…?
- your vision
- your hearing
- talking/your speech

- su visión
- su oído/audición
- su habla

Do you take medications?   ¿Usted toma medicamentos/medicaciones?

Social History

Do you exercise?   ¿Hace ejercicio?

How often do you exercise?   ¿Con qué frecuencia hace ejercicio?

Where do you live?   ¿Dónde vive?

In an apartment or a house?	¿En un apartamento o en una casa?
Are there stairs in your house?	¿Hay escalones/escaleras en su casa?
How many stairs are there?	¿Cuántas escaleras hay?
How many floors do you have in your house?	¿Cuántos pisos tiene su casa? ¿Cuántos pisos hay en su casa?
Where is…? or On what floor is…?	¿Dónde está…? o ¿En qué piso está…?
• the kitchen	• la cocina
• your room	• su habitación, su dormitorio, su cuarto
• the bathroom	• el baño
• the telephone	• el teléfono
Does anyone live with you?	¿Vive alguien con usted?
With whom do you live?	¿Con quién vive?
Are you…?	¿Es…? o ¿Está…?
• married	• casado(a)
• single	• soltero(a)
• widowed	• viudo(a)
Do you work?	¿Usted trabaja?
Where do you work?	¿Dónde trabaja?
What type of work do you do?	¿Qué tipo de trabajo hace? ¿Qué tipo de trabajo tiene?
What do you do for work?	¿Qué hace en su trabajo?

Determining Equipment Needs

Do you use…? <u>or</u> Do you have…?

- any equipment…
  - to walk
  - to shower
- a wheelchair
- a cane
- a walker…

  - with wheels
  - without wheels
  - with a seat

Did you need help…? <u>or</u> How much help did you need…?

- in your house
- before you were admitted
- to walk
- to get up
- to go up the stairs
- to go down the stairs
- to lie down
- to stand
- to move yourself

And now, do you need help…?

- in your house
- to walk
- to get up
- to go up the stairs
- to go down the stairs

¿Usa…? <u>o</u> ¿Tiene…?

- algún equipo…
  - para caminar
  - para ducharse
- silla de ruedas
- un bastón
- una caminadora…, un andador…

  - con ruedas
  - sin ruedas
  - con silla

¿Necesitó ayuda…? <u>o</u> ¿Cuánta ayuda necesitó…?

- en su casa
- antes de que fuera ingresado
- para caminar, para andar
- para levantarse
- para subir las escaleras
- para bajar las escaleras
- para acostarse
- para pararse, para mantenerse de pie
- para moverse

¿Y ahora, necesita ayuda…?

- en su casa
- para caminar, para andar
- para levantarse
- para subir las escaleras
- para bajar las escaleras

- to lie down
- to stand
- to move yourself

- para acostarse
- para pararse, para mantenerse de pie
- para moverse

A lot or a little?

¿Mucho o poco?

To Better Understand the Patient

I don't understand.

No comprendo/entiendo.

Please, repeat that.

Por favor, repita eso.
Por favor, repita lo que dijo.

I am sorry.

Lo siento.

Excuse me.

Discúlpeme.

Pardon me.

Perdóneme.

Speak slowly.

Hable más lento.

Calm down.

Cálmese.

You will be okay.

Usted se pondrá bien.
Usted estará bien.

Determining the Problem

What happened?

¿Qué ocurrió?

How did you hurt it/yourself?

¿Cómo se lastimó?

Do you have/feel weakness in any part of your body?

¿Tiene/Siente debilidad en alguna parte de su cuerpo?

Questions about Pain

Where does it hurt?	¿Dónde le duele?
Show me where it hurts.	Dígame/Muéstreme dónde le duele.
Point to the part of the body where it hurts.	Señale la parte del cuerpo dónde le duele.
What hurts?	¿Qué le duele? ¿Qué molestias tiene?

Do you have pain when you…? ¿Tiene dolor cuándo…?

- walk
- drive
- chew
- get up/rise
- go up the stairs
- go down the stairs
- sleep
- lie down
- stand

- move oneself

- anda, camina
- conduce, maneja
- mastica
- se levanta
- sube las escaleras
- baja las escaleras
- duerme, al dormir
- se acuesta
- al pararse, se para, se mantiene en pie
- al moverse, se mueve

What bothers you?	¿Qué le molesta?
Is anything bothering you?	¿Hay algo que le molesta? ¿Le molesta algo?
How much pain do you have?	¿Cuánto dolor tiene? ¿Qué tanto le duele? ¿Cuánto le duele?

Evaluation: The Questions

On a scale from 0 to 10, zero is no pain and ten is a lot of pain and it is necessary to go to the hospital, how much pain do you have?	En una escala de cero a diez, cero es no dolor y diez es mucho dolor y necesita ir al hospital, ¿Cuánto dolor tiene?
On a scale of 0 to 10, with 10 being the worst, what is your pain number?	¿En una escala de cero a diez, donde diez es el peor dolor, en qué número está su dolor?
Now?	¿Ahora?
When you rest?	¿Cuándo descansa?
With activity/movement?	¿Con actividad/movimiento?
What type of pain is it?	¿Qué tipo de dolor es?
What type of pain do you have?	¿Qué tipo de dolor tiene?
Do you have ____ pain? or Is the pain...?	¿Tiene dolor...? o ¿Es el dolor...?

- constant
- intermittent
- mild
- moderate
- increasing
- the same
- decreasing

- constante
- intermitente
- templado/leve
- moderado
- aumentando
- igual
- disminuyendo

Does the pain come and go?	¿El dolor va y viene?
When did the pain start/begin?	¿Cuándo comenzó/empezó el dolor?
When did you start to have the pain?	¿Cuándo comenzó a tener dolor?

When did you start to feel the pain?	¿Cuándo comenzó a sentir el dolor?
How long have you had the pain?	¿Cuánto tiempo ha tenido el dolor?
Do you feel the pain all the time?	¿Siente el dolor todo el tiempo?
How often?	¿Con qué frecuencia?
How often does it occur?	¿Cada cuánto le sucede? ¿Cada cuánto le pasa?
What brings it on?	¿Qué es lo que [se] lo provoca?
What makes the pain…? • better • worse	¿Qué hace el dolor sea…? • mejor • peor
What makes the pain better?	¿Qué le alivia el dolor?
What makes the pain worse?	¿Qué empeora el dolor?
How have you tried to alleviate the problem?	¿Cómo ha tratado de aliviar el problema?
Does it hurt when you touch it?	¿Le duele cuándo se lo(la) toca?
Does it hurt when I touch it?	¿Le duele cuándo lo(la) toco?
Have you had this pain before?	¿Ha sentido este dolor antes?

Note - see the pain section in vocabulary for a more complete list of pain symptoms and types of pain.

Head and Neck

Do you have headaches frequently?	¿Tiene dolor de cabeza con frecuencia?
How often?	¿Cada cuánto?
How long do they last?	¿Cuánto tiempo le dura el dolor?
Does it hurt when you turn your head?	¿Le duele al voltear la cabeza?
Does your pain radiate to your arm?	¿El dolor se extiende por su brazo? ¿El dolor se irradia a su brazo?

Shoulder

Are you able to reach behind your back? — ¿Puede alcanzar hacia atrás de su espalda?

Are you able to dress yourself without help? — ¿Puede vestirse sin ayuda?

Are you able…? — ¿Puede…?

- to zip up your zipper
  - subirse la bragueta/el cierre/la cremallera/el zipper
  - cerrarse la bragueta/el cierre/la cremallera/el zipper
- to button your shirt
  - abotonarse la camisa/camiseta
  - abrocharse la camisa/camiseta

- to tie your shoelaces
- amarrarse/atarse los zapatos

Are you able to throw objects? ¿Puede tirar/lanzar objetos?

Are you able to drive? ¿Puede conducir/manejar?

Back

Are you able to bend your back…? ¿Puede doblar su espalda…?
- forward
- backwards
- to the right
- to the left

- hacia adelante
- hacia atrás
- a la derecha
- a la izquierda

Are you able to turn…? ¿Puede voltear/girar…?
- to the right
- to the left

- a la derecha
- a la izquierda

For how many minutes can you…? ¿Por cuántos minutos puede…?
- stand
- sit

- estar de pie, estar parado
- estar sentado

Does your pain radiate to your leg? ¿El dolor se extiende por su pierna?
¿El dolor se irradia a su pierna?

Knee

Are you able to bend your knee? ¿Puede doblar su rodilla?

Are you able to straighten your knee?

¿Puede enderezar/estirar su rodilla?

Cardiorespiratory

Do you have difficulty breathing?

¿Tiene alguna dificultad para respirar?

Do you have shortness of breath?

¿Siente que le falta el aire?
¿Tiene falta de respiración?

Does your chest hurt when you breathe?

¿Le duele el pecho al respirar?

Is the pain worse when you breathe?

¿Se hace el dolor más fuerte cuándo respira?

Do you have problems with your heart?

¿Tiene algún problema en el corazón?

Do you have a pacemaker?

¿Tiene un marcapasos?

Musculoskeletal

Do you feel weakness in…?
- your body
- your arm
- your leg

¿Siente debilidad en…?
- su cuerpo
- su brazo
- su pierna

Do you have any problems in your joints?

¿Tiene algún problema en las coyunturas/articulaciones?

Do your joints swell or redden?

¿Se le hinchan o enrojecen las coyunturas/articulaciones?

Do your joints get stiff?	¿Se le ponen tiesas las articulaciones/coyunturas?
Do you have arthritis?	¿Tiene artritis?

Nervous System

Do you feel weakness in any part of your body?	¿Siente debilidad en alguna parte del cuerpo?
Is there a part of your body…?	¿Hay alguna parte de su cuerpo…?
• that you are not able to move	• que no puede mover
• that you don't feel	• que no siente
Do you have seizures?	¿Ha tenido ataques/convulsiones?

Pediatrics

Can your child…?	¿Su niño puede…?
• move his/her hands and legs	• mover los brazos y las piernas
• lift and maintain the head up when lying on the stomach	• levantar y mantener la cabeza arriba cuándo está acostado boca abajo
• reach for objects	• tratar de alcanzar/agarrar objetos
• roll from stomach to back	• voltearse del estómago a la espalda, voltearse boca arriba

- roll from back to stomach
- roll onto the side
- sit…
  - with help
  - without help
- get into standing…
  - with help
  - without help
- crawl
- go up on the knees
- kneel
- half kneel
- stand…
  - with help
  - without help
- walk…
  - with help
  - without help
- step off a step and keep his/her balance
- walk up the stairs putting both feet on a step
- walk up and down stairs alternating feet
- ride a tricycle
- ride a bike
- stand on one foot?
- jump

- voltearse de la espalda al estómago, voltearse boca abajo
- voltearse de lado
- sentarse…
  - con ayuda
  - sin ayuda
- se pone de pie apoyándose…
  - con ayuda
  - sin ayuda
- gatear con las manos y las rodillas
- subir las rodillas
- arrodillarse
- medio arrodillarse
- pararse…, mantenerse en pie…
  - con ayuda
  - sin ayuda
- caminar…, andar…
  - con ayuda
  - sin ayuda
- bajar las escaleras y mantener el equilibrio
- subir las escaleras poniendo ambos pies en el mismo escalón
- subir y bajar las gradas/ escaleras poniendo cada pie en un escalón
- montar/andar en triciclo
- montar/andar en una bicicleta
- pararse en un pie, mantenerse en un pie
- saltar

- jump on one foot
- jump from a step
- skip

- saltar en un pie, saltar sobre un pie
- saltar de la grada, saltar del escalón
- brincar en un pie

Red Flags

Have you had an unexpected weight gain?	¿Ha aumentado de peso inesperadamente?
Have you had an unexpected weight loss?	¿Ha tenido una pérdida de peso inesperada?
When you use the bathroom, do you have blood in your urine or stool?	¿Cuándo usa el baño tiene sangre en sus excrementos u orina?

Note - There are other red flags not listed in this section.

Smoke Cessation

You have to stop smoking.	Tiene que dejar de fumar.
Do you need help to stop smoking?	¿Necesita ayuda para dejar de fumar?

Notes

5

The Examination: Measurements

This chapter focuses on objective measurements, such as vital signs, range of motion, and strength testing. The sections on head and neck, shoulder, back, knee, and foot have specific commands on getting patients into certain positions. From there, the therapist can test the patient's strength or obtain their range of motion measurements. The therapist may also find it more beneficial to demonstrate the movements as patients may not fully understand the instructions.

The Basics

I need you to undress.

Necesito que se desvista.
Necesito quitarle la ropa.

Do not remove… <u>or</u> Leave ____ on.
- the underwear
- the shorts
- the bra

No se quite… <u>o</u> Quédese con ____ [puesta].
- la ropa interior
- los shorts/los pantalones cortos
- el sostén

Put this gown on.

Póngase esta bata.

May I touch you?

¿Puedo tocarlo(la)?

The Examination: Measurements

I'm going to take…
- your vital signs
- your pulse
- your blood pressure
- your oxygen levels

Le voy a tomar…
- sus signos vitales
- el pulso
- la presión arterial
- sus niveles del oxígeno

I need to measure the range of motion of…
- your arm
- your leg

Necesito medir el rango de movimiento de…
- su brazo
- su pierna

I need to measure the movement of…
- your elbow
- your foot

Necesito medir el movimiento de…
- su codo
- su pie

I would like to test your strength.

Me gustaría examinar su fuerza.
Me gustaría hacerle una prueba de fuerza.

Resist me.

Resístase.
Ponga resistencia.

Hold this position.

Mantenga esta posición.

Do not move.

No se mueva.

Don't let me move you.

No me deje moverlo.
No deje que lo mueva.

Hold for [insert number]…
- seconds
- minutes

Manténgalo(la) por/durante [#]…
- segundos
- minutos

As much as you are able [to].

Lo más que pueda.

Head and Neck

Look up at the ceiling.	Mire arriba al techo.
Move your head up toward the ceiling.	Mueva la cabeza hacia arriba al techo.
Look down toward the floor.	Mire abajo al piso/suelo.
Move your head down toward the chest.	Mueva la cabeza hacia abajo al pecho.

Turn…
- to the left
- to the right

Voltee/Gire…
- a la izquierda
- a la derecha

Bring your ear toward your shoulder.	Traiga su oído hacia su hombro.

Bend your neck…
- to the left
- to the right

Doble su cuello…
- a la izquierda
- a la derecha

Shoulder

Lift your hand up toward the ceiling.	Levante el brazo adelante hacia el techo.
Lift your hand out to the side and up.	Levante el brazo al lado y hacia arriba.

Lift your shoulder to the side to [insert number] degrees. Keep the elbow bent and bring your forearm up [ER].	Levante el hombro al lado a nivel de [#] grados. Mantenga el codo doblado y ponga el antebrazo arriba [rotación externa].
Lift your shoulder to the side to [insert number] degrees. Keep the elbow bent and bring your forearm down [IR].	Levante el hombro al lado a nivel de [#] grados. Mantenga el codo doblado y ponga el antebrazo abajo [rotación interna].

Note - For internal and external rotation, it may be easier to demonstrate this motion as it may be confusing to the patient.

Back

Bend...	Dóblese...
	Agáchese...
	Inclínese...
• forward	• hacia adelante, hacia el frente
Bend...	Dóblese...
	Inclínese...
• backwards	• hacia atrás
• to the right	• a la derecha
• to the left	• a la izquierda
Turn to the right.	Voltéese/Gire a la derecha.
Turn to the left.	Voltéese/Gire a la izquierda.

Knee

Bend your knee.   Doble su rodilla.

Straighten your knee.   Enderece/Estire la rodilla.

Foot

Bring the foot… or Move the foot…
- up
- down
- in/inside
- out

Ponga el pie… o Mueva el pie…
- arriba
- abajo
- adentro
- afuera

For more commands and instructions, see commands in Plan of Care chapter.

Notes

6

Reevaluation: Revisit Questions

This chapter should be used when reevaluating a patient. This chapter only focuses on questions and statements that were not asked in the previous chapters 4 and 5. Please review the previous two chapters, as many questions or statements from the previous chapters can also be used when reevaluating a patient.

Reevaluation Questions

Since you started therapy, do you feel better, the same, or worse [with therapy]?

¿Desde que usted empezó la terapia, se siente mejor, igual, o peor [con la terapia]?

Do you want to continue with therapy?

¿Usted quiere seguir con la terapia?

Do you feel you can do your exercises at home?

¿Puede hacer los ejercicios en casa?

You do not need to continue therapy.

No necesita seguir/continuar con la terapia.
No es necesario que siga/continúe con la terapia.

I recommend that you return to your doctor because…

Le recomiendo que vuelva a ver a su doctor porque…

- therapy has not helped
- you have too much pain
- you still have pain
- your range of motion has not changed
- you are getting worse

- la terapia no le ha ayudado
- tiene mucho dolor
- todavía tiene dolor
- no ha cambiado el rango de movimiento
- usted se está poniendo peor

Your ____ has improved with therapy.
- strength
- movement
- pain level

Ha mejorado su ____ con la terapia.
- fuerza
- movimiento
- nivel de dolor

You need to do your home exercise program.

Necesita hacer su ejercicio [de terapia] en su casa.

We will continue with therapy…
- one time a week
- two times a week
- every two weeks

Vamos a seguir/continuar con la terapia…
- una vez a la semana
- dos veces por semana
- cada dos semanas

Notes

7

Plan of Care

This chapter can be used to assist in scheduling appointments and to develop a treatment plan, if further therapy is warranted, after the evaluation.

Making an Appointment

Do you have an appointment?	¿Usted tiene una cita?
Do you need to make an appointment?	¿Necesita hacer una cita?
What day(s) are you able to have [physical] therapy?	¿Qué día(s) puede realizar la terapia [física]?

Come back and see me...
- inside of two weeks
- in two days

Vuelva a verme...
- dentro de dos semanas
- en dos días

We'll see you in...
- a day
- a week
- a month

Nos vemos en...
- un día
- una semana
- un mes

Note - *The reader is able to choose a specific day or month from the days of the week, or the months of the year. - See the first chapter.*

You do not need therapy.	No necesita terapia.
You need to exercise…	Necesita hacer ejercicio…
• to increase your movement	• para aumentar su movimiento
• to increase your strength	• para aumentar su fuerza
You need to join a gym.	Necesita ir al gimnasio.
You need to take…	Necesita tomar…
• exercise classes	• clases de ejercicios
• water aerobics	• aeróbicos acuáticos, aeróbicos en el agua
• yoga	• yoga
range of motion exercises [ROM]	los ejercicios de rango de movimiento

Commands

Show me.	Muéstreme.
Bend…	Doble…
• your elbow	• su codo
Straighten…	Enderece… Estire…
• your knee	• su rodilla
Lie down.	Acuéstese.

Grab...
- the bar

Put your weight...
- on your foot

Do not put your weight...
- on your knee

Go up the stairs.

Go down the stairs.

Be careful.

Relax.

Hold for [insert number]...

- seconds
- minutes

Pull...
- the shirt down

Push...
- the door

Exhale.

Extend...
- the arm

Please get on the scale.

Do this.

Agarre...
- la barra

Apóyese...
- en su pie

No se apoye...
- en su rodilla

Suba las escaleras.

Baje las escaleras.

Tenga cuidado.

Relájese.
Tranquilo.

Manténgalo(la) por/durante [#]...

- segundos
- minutos

Jale...
- la camiseta abajo

Empuje...
- la puerta

Exhale.

Extienda/Estire...
- el brazo

Por favor suba a la báscula.

Haga esto(a).

Lean...
- forward

Put _____ together...
- your feet

Get up.

Don't get up.

Keep it straight.
  e.g. Keep your back straight.

Show me.

Put on the gown.

Move your arm.

Don't worry.

Sit down.

Don't sit down.

Come here.

Turn...

Inclínese...
- hacia adelante

Junte...
- los pies

Levántese.

No se levante.

Manténgala derecha.
  e.g. Mantenga su espalda derecha/recta.

Muéstreme.

Póngase la bata.

Mueva el brazo.

No se preocupe.

Siéntese.

No se siente.

Venga aquí.
Venga acá.

Voltéese...
Dese la vuelta...

Notes

8

Verbs

Please review the verb tenses and conjugations if you have problems conjugating verbs. Many verbs have irregular tenses and it is important to familiarize yourself with these verbs.

Notes

A

to accept - aceptar

to accompany - acompañar

to admit [to hospital] - ingresar

to alleviate - aliviar

to amputate - amputar

to annoy someone - molestar

to answer - contestar, responder

to arrive - llegar

to ask - pedir, preguntar

Notes

to ask a question - hacer una pregunta

to attend - asistir

to avoid - evitar

B

to balance - balancear

to bathe oneself [take a bath] - bañarse

to bathe someone - bañar

to be - estar, ser

to be able [can] - poder

to be annoyed - molestarse

to be called - llamarse

to be lacking/missing - faltar

to be late - tardar, llegar tarde

to be named - llamarse

to be pregnant - estar embarazada

to beat - golpear, pegar

Notes

to become pregnant - embarazarse, quedar embarazada

to begin - comenzar, empezar

to believe - creer

to bend - doblar, inclinar

to bend down/over - agacharse, doblarse

to bite - morder

to bleed - sangrar

to bother - molestar

to break - romper

to breathe - respirar

to bring - traer

to buckle - abrocharse

to bump - tropezar

to burn - quemar

to button [up] - abotonarse

to buy - comprar

Notes

C

to call - llamar

to calm oneself - calmarse

to calm someone - calmar

to care for oneself - cuidarse

to care for someone - cuidar

to carry - llegar

to catch - coger

to cause - causar

to change - cambiar

to chat - charlar

to chew - masticar

to choose - escoger, elegir

to circulate - circular

to clean - limpiar

to close - cerrar

to come - venir

to command - mandar

to complete - completar

Notes

to consult - consultar

to contaminate - contaminar

to continue - continuar, seguir

to cook - cocinar

to count - contar

to crash - chocar

to crawl - gatear

to cry - llorar

to cure - curar

to cut - cortar

D

to decrease - disminuir

to defecate - defecar

to deny - negar

to describe - describir

to desire - desear

to develop - desarrollar

Notes

to disinfect - desinfectar

to do - hacer

to do up - abrochar

to double - doblar

to dress - vestir

to dress oneself - vestirse

to drink - beber, tomar [una bebida]

to drive - conducir, manejar

to dry - secar

E

to earn - ganar

to eat - comer

to end - terminar

to enjoy - disfrutar, gozar

to enter - entrar

to evaluate - evaluar

to examine - examinar

to exercise - ejercer, hacer ejercicio

Notes

to exhale - exhalar

to explain - explicar

to extend - extender

F

to faint - desmayar

to fall - caer

to fasten - abrochar

to feel - sentir [sorry], sentirse
   [well, ill]

to fill, fill out - llenar

to find - encontrar, hallar

to fit into - caber

to follow - seguir

to forget - olvidar

to fracture - fracturar

<u>**Notes**</u>

G

to gain - ganar

to gather - recoger

to get - conseguir, obtener, sacar

to get married - casarse

to get sick - enfermarse

to get up [rise] - levantar

to give - dar

to go - ir

to go down [lower] - bajar

   e.g. to lose weight - bajar de peso

to go out - salir

to go to bed - acostarse

to go up - subir

to grab - agarrar, coger, tomar

to grow - crecer

to guard - vigilar

Notes

H

to happen - ocurrir, suceder

to have - tener, haber

to have breakfast - desayunar

to have dinner - cenar

to have lunch - almorzar

to have to - tener que

to hear - oír

to help - ayudar

to hit - golpear, pegar

to hope - esperar

to hospitalize - internar

to hurt - dañar, doler, herir, lastimar

to hurt oneself - lastimarse

I

to immunize - inmunizar, vacunar

to improve - mejorar

Notes

to increase - aumentar, crecer

to indicate - indicar

to infect - contagiar

to inhale - inhalar

to inject - inyectar

to irrigate - irrigar

to isolate - aislar

J

to jog - trotar

to join - juntar

to jump - saltar

K

to keep - guardar

to kick - patear

to kneel - arrodillarse

to know - conocer [someone],

   saber [a fact]

Notes

L

to last - durar

to lean - inclinar

to learn - aprender

to leave - salir

to leave behind - dejar de

   e.g. to quit smoking - dejar de fumar

to let - dejar

to lie down - acostarse

to lift [up] - levantar

to like - gustar

to listen to - escuchar

to live - vivir

to look [at] - mirar

to look for - buscar

to lose - perder

Notes

M

to maintain - mantener, sostener

to make - hacer

to make an appointment - citar

to march - marchar

to marry - casarse

to massage - masajear

to measure - medir

to meet - encontrar

to miss - faltar

to mount - montar

to move - mover

to move oneself - moverse

N

to name - llamar

to need - necesitar

Notes

O

to observe - observar

to obtain - obtener

to occur - ocurrir, suceder

to open - abrir

to operate - operar

to order - mandar [something], ordenar

to ought to - deber

P

to park - estacionar

to pass [time] - pasar

to pay - pagar

to pedal [a bike] - pedalear

to perform - realizar

to pick up - recoger

to point out - señalar

Notes

to practice - practicar

to pray - rezar

to prepare - preparar

to prescribe - recetar

to provoke - provocar

to pull - jalar, tirar

to push - empujar

to put - poner

to put a cast on - enyesar

to put on [clothes] - ponerse

to put someone to bed - acostar

to put together - juntar

Q

to question - preguntar

R

to radiate - irradiar

to raise - levantar

Notes

to reach - alcanzar

to read - leer

to readmit - readmitir

to receive - recibir

to recommend - recomendar

to regret - sentir

to relax - relajar

to release - soltar

to remain - quedar

to remember - acordarse, recodar[se]

to remove - quitar

to repeat - repetir

to replace - reemplazar

to resist - resistir

to rest - descansar

to return - regresar, volver

to ride [e.g. a bike] - andar,

   montar [e.g. en una bicicleta]

Notes

to rinse - enjuagar

to run - correr

S

to save [a life] - salvar

to say - decir

to see - ver

to seem - parecer

to sell - vender

to send - enviar, mandar

to separate - separar

to shout - gritar

to show - mostrar, señalar

to shower - duchar

to shower oneself - ducharse

to sign - firmar

to signify - significar

to sit - sentar

to sit oneself - sentarse

Notes

to skip - brincar

to slap - abofetear

to sleep - dormir

to smoke - fumar

to speak - hablar

to spend [time] - pasar

to spend - gastar

to spit - escupir

to sprain - torcer

to spread - contagiar

to squeeze - apretar

to stand - estar de pie, pararse

to start - comenzar, empezar

to stay - quedar

to sterilize - esterilizar

to stop - parar, detener

to stop oneself - pararse

to straighten - enderezar

Notes

to stretch - estirar

to strike - pegar

to suck - chupar

to suffer - sufrir

to support - mantener, sostener

to support oneself - apoyarse

to suppose to - deber

to swallow - tragar

to swell - hinchar

to swim - nadar

T

to take - coger, tomar, agarrar

to take care of - cuidar, guardar

to take [clothing] off oneself - quitarse

to take out - sacar

to talk - hablar

to taste - probar

Notes

to teach - enseñar

to tear - romper

to tell - contar, decir

to terminate - terminar

to think - pensar

to throw - echar, tirar, lanzar

to tie - atarse, amarrarse

to tighten - apretar

to touch - tocar

to travel - viajar

to treat, to try - tratar

to try to - tratar de

to turn - voltear, girar

to turn around onself - voltearse

to turn off [e.g. lights] - apagar

to turn on [e.g. lights] - encender,
   prender

Notes

to turn red - enrojecer

to twist - torcer

U

to understand - comprender, entender

to undress - desvestir

to undress oneself - desvestirse

to urinate - orinar

to use - usar

to utilize - utilizar

V

to vaccinate - vacunar

to visit - visitar

W

to wait [for] - esperar

to wake oneself up - despertarse

to wake up someone - despertar

Notes

to walk - andar, caminar

to want - querer, desear

to wash oneself - lavarse

to wash something - lavar

to watch - mirar, vigilar

to wear - llevar

to weight - pesar

to wet - mojar

to work - trabajar

to worry oneself - preocuparse

to worsen - empeorar

to wound - herir

to write - escribir

CPSIA information can be obtained
at www.ICGtesting.com
Printed in the USA
LVOW04s0350030516

486409LV00007B/23/P